NEW YORK KNICKS

ALL-TIME GREATS

BY TED COLEMAN

Book design by Jake Slavik
Cover design by Jake Slavik

Photographs ©: David Zalubowski/AP Images, cover (top), 1 (top); AP Images, cover (bottom), 1 (bottom), 4, 9, 10; Ed Kolenovsky/AP Images, 6; Bill Kostroun/AP Images, 12, 18; Carlos Osorio/AP Images, 15; Frank Franklin II/AP Images, 16; Noah K. Murray/AP Images, 21

Press Box Books, an imprint of Press Room Editions.

ISBN
978-1-63494-604-9 (library bound)
978-1-63494-622-3 (paperback)
978-1-63494-640-7 (epub)
978-1-63494-656-8 (hosted ebook)

Library of Congress Control Number: 2022913241

Distributed by North Star Editions, Inc.
2297 Waters Drive
Mendota Heights, MN 55120
www.northstareditions.com

Printed in the United States of America
Mankato, MN
012023

ABOUT THE AUTHOR

Ted Coleman is a freelance sportswriter and children's book author who lives in Louisville, Kentucky, with his trusty Affenpinscher, Chloe.

TABLE OF CONTENTS

REED
19
NEW YORK
19

CHAPTER 1
THE GOLDEN ERA

The New York Knickerbockers were founded in 1946. They made the playoffs a lot in their early years. A big reason why was the play of point guard **Dick McGuire**. "Tricky Dick" began running the Knicks' offense in 1949. McGuire helped the Knicks reach the NBA Finals three times.

McGuire left in 1957. The Knicks soon started losing. But **Willis Reed** turned that around. The powerful center was the NBA's Rookie of the Year in 1965. And he never slowed down. Reed was a scoring and

FRAZIER
10

rebounding force for 10 seasons. He was also tough. The 1970 NBA Finals came down to Game 7. Reed had a torn muscle in his right leg. Still, he led the Knicks to their first NBA title.

Forward **Bill Bradley** was known for his vision on the court. Bradley seemed to think two or three passes ahead. Bradley never put up huge numbers. But he was a key part of the Knicks' core of this era.

Running the offense was **Walt Frazier**. The former high school quarterback made all the right moves. The Knicks made the playoffs in each of his first eight seasons. Frazier

STAT SPOTLIGHT

CAREER ASSISTS

KNICKS TEAM RECORD

Walt Frazier: 4,791

became the Knicks' all-time leader in several categories, including points.

Earl "The Pearl" Monroe was one of the most stylish players in basketball. His slick passes and athletic moves left fans in awe. Bradley called him a "playground player." He just had fun when he was playing.

RED HOLZMAN

William "Red" Holzman was a champion as a player. Then he became a coach. And he demanded the same level of greatness. Holzman coached the Knicks' two NBA titles in the 1970s. He built teams that played tough defense above all else. Holzman believed defense led to good offense. His 613 wins are the most in Knicks history.

The Knicks could play defense, too. **Dave DeBusschere** was as fierce as they come. He made the NBA All-Defensive First Team in the first six years it existed. Teammates and fans loved the effort he gave each night.

The Knicks won NBA titles in 1970 and 1973. And all five key players had their jersey numbers retired. This era remains the most successful in Knicks history.

KING
30
NEW YORK
30

CHAPTER 2

EWING ARRIVES

By the early 1980s, the Knicks' championship era had passed. But forward **Bernard King** was there to thrill fans. King was known for his explosive scoring ability. The All-Star once had two straight 50-point games.

King and center **Bill Cartwright** formed a great duo. The 7'1" Cartwright was a rebounding force under the hoop. However, both players were hurt in the 1984–85 season. New York was one of the worst teams in the league. But there was a bright side. The Knicks ended up with the first overall draft pick.

They used it to take another powerful center. **Patrick Ewing** had been a star in college. He brought the same dominance to New York.

Ewing set almost every major Knicks record. In 15 seasons with the Knicks, he made 11 All-Star teams. Ewing led the Knicks to the

1994 NBA Finals. He averaged 21.7 points and 11.7 rebounds per game during the playoff run. But it wasn't enough. New York lost to the Houston Rockets.

The Knicks worked to build a talented team around Ewing. Power forward **Charles Oakley** brought toughness and scoring. Oakley and Ewing were a nightmare duo for opponents.

Guard **John Starks** wasn't even drafted by an NBA team. But he played his way into a starter. Just 6'3", Starks had to work hard to keep his place on the court. Starks was a great

STAT SPOTLIGHT

CAREER POINTS

KNICKS TEAM RECORD

Patrick Ewing: 23,665

three-point shooter. He made more threes than anyone in team history.

Few Knicks players can match the success of guard **Allan Houston**. Houston ranked fourth behind Ewing, Walt Frazier, and Willis Reed in points scored. One of his shots was the most memorable of all. He hit a game-winner in a 1999 playoff game. The Knicks went on to make the NBA Finals.

But Ewing got hurt during the playoffs. The Knicks fell short again. They lost to the San Antonio Spurs in five games.

PAT RILEY

Pat Riley coached the Knicks for just four seasons. But 1991 to 1995 was one of the best periods in team history. New York won 50 games or more each season. The 1993–94 team knocked off the defending champions, the Chicago Bulls. Riley left with the best winning percentage of any Knicks coach.

NEW YORK
20
HOUSTON
20

STOUDEMIRE
1
NEW YORK
1

CHAPTER 3
NEW GENERATION

There was no question it would be hard to replace Patrick Ewing. The team tried to add star veterans to improve quickly. Point guard **Stephon Marbury** arrived in a 2004 trade. The New York native was a playmaker. He could get the Knicks offense running.

But Marbury led the team to just one playoff appearance before he left in 2009. The Knicks shifted to a fast-paced offense. The key player was **Amar'e Stoudemire**.

The 6'10" Stoudemire came to New York in 2010. He was already an All-Star. His strengths

were scoring and rebounding. Stoudemire helped turn the Knicks back into a playoff contender. He averaged more than 25 points per game in his first season in New York. But

LINSANITY

On February 4, 2012, Jeremy Lin came off the bench to score 25 points in a win. Days later, the undrafted point guard scored 28 points in another win. Lin provided a spark for a Knicks team that had lost 11 of 13 games. Soon, Lin was starting. In fact, he turned around the team's entire season. The Knicks went on the make the playoffs as "Linsanity" took over New York.

injuries prevented him from hitting that mark again.

The addition of forward **Carmelo Anthony** in 2011 added even more scoring. It was a big move for Anthony. He was traded from the Denver Nuggets. Anthony led the league in scoring in 2012–13. He steadily climbed the Knicks' scoring leaderboards.

STAT SPOTLIGHT

POINTS IN A GAME

KNICKS TEAM RECORD

Carmelo Anthony: 62 (January 24, 2014)

However, the team won just a single playoff series with him.

That win in 2013 was the last time the Knicks made the playoffs until 2021. The team's hopes then relied on a young player and a veteran. **RJ Barrett** was New York's top draft pick in 2019. Barrett started off slow. But by 2020–21, he was a fixture in the lineup.

The veteran was **Julius Randle**. Randle hadn't made much of an impact in the first five seasons of his career. He came to the Knicks in 2019. In 2020–21, he won the league's Most Improved Player Award. His play helped the Knicks return to the playoffs. Fans hoped they had two stars to build around for the future.

Wilson
YORK
30
KLEBER
42
RANDLE
30

TIMELINE

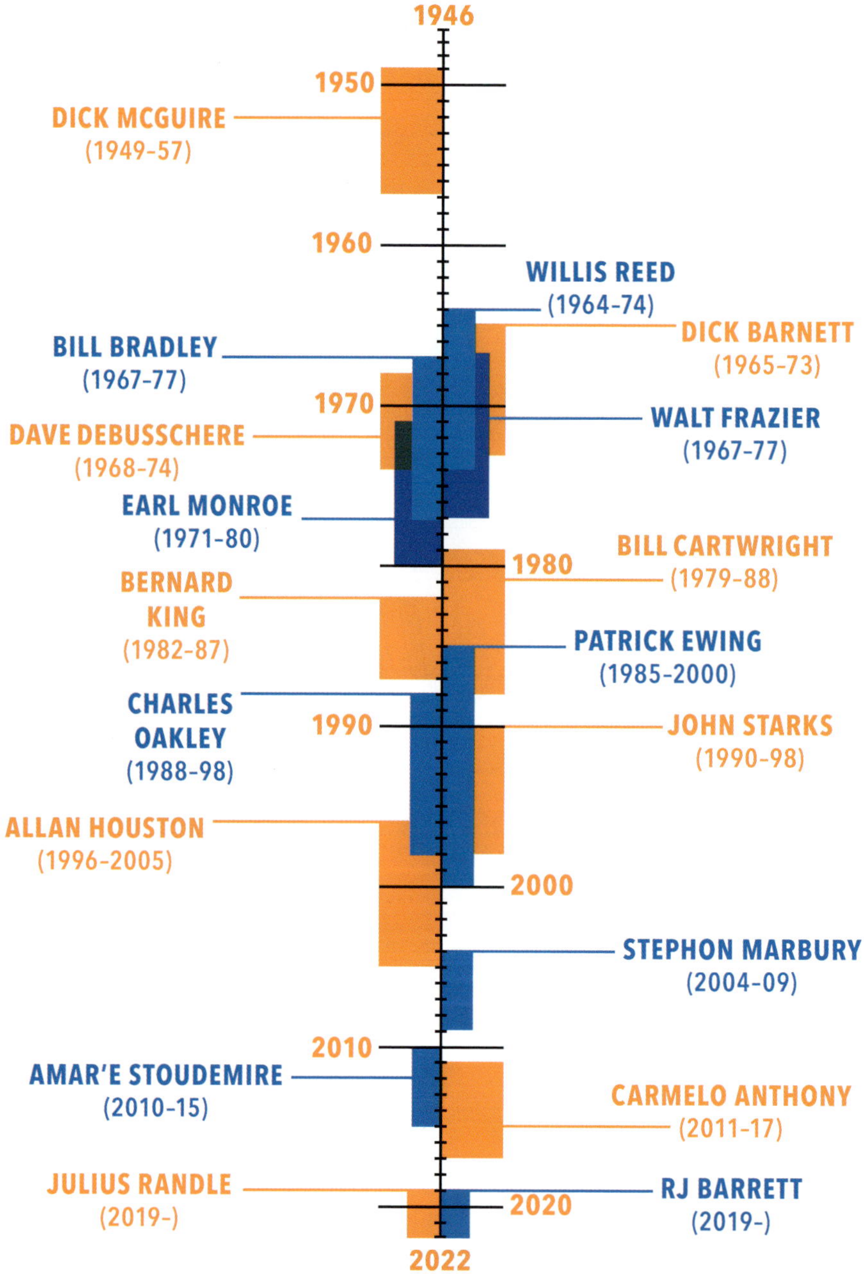
1946
1950
DICK MCGUIRE
(1949-57)
1960
WILLIS REED
(1964-74)
DICK BARNETT
(1965-73)
BILL BRADLEY
(1967-77)
1970
DAVE DEBUSSCHERE
(1968-74)
WALT FRAZIER
(1967-77)
EARL MONROE
(1971-80)
BILL CARTWRIGHT
1980
(1979-88)
BERNARD KING
(1982-87)
PATRICK EWING
(1985-2000)
CHARLES OAKLEY
(1988-98)
1990
JOHN STARKS
(1990-98)
ALLAN HOUSTON
(1996-2005)
2000
STEPHON MARBURY
(2004-09)
2010
AMAR'E STOUDEMIRE
(2010-15)
CARMELO ANTHONY
(2011-17)
JULIUS RANDLE
(2019-)
RJ BARRETT
2020
(2019-)
2022

TEAM FACTS

NEW YORK KNICKS

First season: 1946–47

NBA championships: 2*

Key coaches:

Red Holzman (1967–68 to 1976–77, 1978–79 to 1981–82)

613–483, 54–43 playoffs, 2 NBA titles

Pat Riley (1991–92 to 1994–95)

223–105, 35–28 playoffs

MORE INFORMATION

To learn more about the New York Knicks, go to **pressboxbooks.com/AllAccess.**

These links are routinely monitored and updated to provide the most current information available.

*Through 2021–22 season

GLOSSARY

contender
A team that is good enough to win a title.

draft
A system that allows teams to acquire new players coming into a league.

era
A period of time in history.

playoffs
A set of games to decide a league's champion.

rookie
A first-year player.

veterans
Players who have spent several years in a league.

INDEX